Table of Contents

Dedication 5

Foreword 7

Introduction 9

    Stages of Grief 10

    Stages of Mourning 11

    Best Practices for Navigating Grief and Loss 16

    Value of Preparation 17

    Managing Grief Triggers 23

    What Not To Say 25

    Let us Pray 29

    Key Definitions 31

    Five Stages of Grief 32

    The Ten Stages of Mourning 33

Day 1 Crucial Transformation 35

Day 2 I AM with You 39

Day 3 Arms Wide Open and Outstretched 43

Day 4 Fight the Good Fight 47

Day 5 Unquenchable Joy is Your Secret Weapon 51

Day 6 You Are My Beloved 55

Day 7 Take Heart and Be Courageous..................................59

Day 8 Be of Good Cheer…..63

Day 9 Walk Boldly Like A Lion..67

Day 10 Calming The Storm..71

Day 11 A New Season Is On The Horizon............................75

Day 12 Peace Is Your Inheritance..79

Day 13 Find The Silver Lining...83

Day 14 Focus On What Truly Counts................................. 87

Day 15 I Press On..91

Day 16 Refocus..95

Day 17 The Fountain of Life...99

Day 18 Crisis of Faith...103

Day 19 Beyond What You Can Ask or Think..................... 107

Day 20 Don't Hesitate.. 111

Day 21 Rest and Recover 115

Day 22 Empowered from Within 119

Day 23 First Things First...123

Day 24 Choose Joy...127

Day 25 Improve Your Quality of Life.................................131

Day 26 Change Course...135

Day 27 An Unbreakable Spiritual Lifeline..139

Day 28 Mindset Shift..143

Day 29 Arise, Encourage Yourself, And Take Off Your Grave Clothes..147

Day 30 Anointed With Fresh Oil...151

Receive Jesus As Savior 155

Receive Holy Spirit..157

Notes...159

Biblical Versions..161

About the Author..163

Contact Information 165

Books By...166

References..167

Dedication

This book is dedicated to my personal Lord and Savior, Jesus Christ, the anchor of my soul.

This hope [this confident assurance] we have as an anchor of the soul [it cannot slip and it cannot break down under whatever pressure bears upon it]—a safe and steadfast hope that enters within the veil [of the heavenly temple, that most Holy Place in which the very presence of God dwells]. **Hebrews 6:19**

Acknowledgment

I am beyond grateful to Tisha Lynton Rose, my homegirl, whose loving support, consistent prayers, prophetic words, proofreading, and encouragement keep me going.

Foreword

It is both an honor and a privilege to write the foreword for this transformative work on managing grief from a biblical perspective, authored by my dear friend and ministry colleague, Dr. Digna Pearson. I have had the joy of knowing Dr. Pearson for eighteen years through our shared ministry at Faith City Central Ministry under the leadership of Apostle Dr. Michael Freeman. Throughout this time, I have witnessed her unwavering commitment to the Word of God, her deep compassion for people, and her dedication to equipping believers with the spiritual tools needed to walk in victory.

As a servant leader, I have faithfully served on the Pastoral Staff and as the Director of Prayer for over 25 years, dedicating my life to intercession, spiritual growth, and equipping believers with the knowledge and authority they need to overcome life's challenges. As an Associate Pastor and author of five books on prayer and the believer's authority, I have had the privilege of mentoring and guiding many in their spiritual walk. In my years of ministry, I have seen firsthand the profound impact of grief on individuals and families, and I understand the necessity of having biblically sound resources to navigate the journey of healing.

Beyond my ministry work, I co-lead a monthly Inspirational Wellness Hour, where I guide individuals through overcoming grief in various areas of life. Whether it's the loss of a loved one, a transition in career or relationships, or any other major life shift, I have helped many find healing through biblical principles, prayer, and practical tools. Having personally walked through my own grief journey after the transition of my mother, I know the importance of intentional focus and a strong spiritual foundation when processing loss.

Why should anyone read this book? Because grief is inevitable, yet few know how to navigate it in a way that brings healing and restoration. This book provides not only biblical truth but also practical tools to help readers live through grief, overcome sorrow, and move forward with grace, joy, and a renewed outlook on life.

I wholeheartedly recommend this book as a powerful resource for those experiencing grief in any form. Dr. Pearson has poured her heart, wisdom, and faith into these pages, and I am confident that this book will bring healing, encouragement, and transformation to many. Dive in with an open heart and mind, apply the wisdom garnered from Dr. Pearson, and watch as the heaviness of grief and sorrow becomes lessened and understanding brings answers and peace.

Pastor Deborah Grant

Introduction

In 2018, both my father and husband transitioned unexpectedly, just eight (8) months apart. I was unprepared for the emotional storm and everything that would follow. On July 4, 2022, four years later, my mother transitioned to heaven as well. Needless to say, I am well acquainted with the concepts of grief and loss that every person encounters in their lifetime. Within the last seven years, I've experienced a wide variety of emotions, ranging from sadness and sorrow to weeping and anger, as well as other overwhelming feelings, which have led to frequent bouts of weeping.

It's essential to recognize that everyone processes and experiences grief and loss in unique ways. According to Howarth (2011), bereavement refers to the transition (loss) of someone as a result of death.[i] Grief is the response to that transition or loss.[ii] It includes various emotional responses and reactions—including anger, fear, and sadness; physiological responses like loss of appetite, inability to sleep, and difficulty breathing; cognitive reactions such as difficulty concentrating, memory issues, and difficulty making decisions; and behavioral responses, including acting out, neglecting oneself, avoidance of others to loss.[iii]

Elisabeth Kubler-Ross developed the five (5) stages of grief, which are used worldwide.[iv] The stages include:

Stage 1: Shock and Denial

This stage occurs upon hearing the initial devastating news, and shock sets in. It is a perfectly normal self-protective mechanism. It is difficult to process the information, and you continue with your normal daily activities because the news is too overwhelming. It can be hard to believe that the events have occurred, and you may refuse to accept the news at this stage, and that's okay.

Stage 2: Anger

As you process the news, anger often emerges, directed toward God, others, and the deceased. This frustration serves as a protective shield for the deep pain of loss. This reaction is a natural part of the grieving process and should be expressed in healthy ways, such as venting to a trusted friend or engaging in physical activities like running.

Stage 3: Bargaining

The stage of bargaining is a desperate attempt to change the outcome and restore what was lost. It is a normal part of the grieving process. During this stage, you are tormented by what you could have done

differently to prevent the loss. It is common to be plagued by what-if scenarios, and it is important to recognize that they are a part of your healing journey.

Stage 4: Depression

Eventually, acceptance of the reality that these circumstances are absolute and unchangeable may lead to withdrawal from normal daily activities and feelings of sadness or depression. This mood or sense of sadness comes and goes, but if it persists for a long period, is ongoing, and includes feelings of hopelessness, please consult a doctor or seek professional help.

Stage 5: Acceptance and Testing

Finally, you arrive at the acceptance and testing stage of grief. It represents a turning point where you have come to terms with the loss and are ready to explore new possibilities and establish a new routine. Boldly embrace the idea of creating a new life for yourself and step out of the shadows of tragedy and loss into a bright future while honoring your past.

Mourning is our cultural response to bereavement and grief and is often marked by meaningful rituals, such as the celebration of life services, wakes, planting a tree, etc.[v] This journey is a process that unfolds in ten (10) distinct stages associated with mourning, each with its

own unique characteristics, emotional challenges, and opportunities for growth:

Stage 1: Shock and denial

Immediately following a loss, an individual initially experiences shock and denial and continues with their daily routine and activities as if nothing has changed. This phase can last from an hour to six weeks. It is a crucial part of the mourning process because it serves as a protective mechanism, allowing time for the reality of the situation to sink in.

Stage 2: Touching contact

In the second stage of mourning, the individual may withdraw from social activities and prefer solitude. This phase, often referred to as the "touching contact" phase, is characterized by a desire for personal space and a reluctance to be physically touched. You may also notice a change in hygienic practices.

Stage 3: Physical symptoms

Grief also manifests physically in some individuals. Physical symptoms include changes in sleeping and eating habits. The mourner may also display or adopt characteristics of the deceased in behavior, illness, and dress.

Stage 4: Alienation

During the fourth stage of mourning, the mourner may exhibit signs of depression, have suicidal thoughts, or engage in substance abuse. Emotional support is critical during the alienation support.

Stage 5: Guilt

As the journey continues, guilt arises. At this stage, individuals may blame themselves for the deceased's death.

Stage 6: Hostility

Anger is a very real and raw emotion during the mourning process. Individuals may deteriorate into angry outbursts, crying, screaming, etc., directed at others or the deceased. It's vital to help the mourner channel these emotions in an appropriate manner.

Stage 7: Perfection

During this stage, the past is idealized. The mourner portrays the circumstances prior to the deceased's transition as perfect or much better than they were. This approach serves as a safeguard against painful emotions, memories, and moments.

Stage 8: Redemption

During the redemptive stage, the mourner no longer feels constrained by grief and eventually transitions to a more positive and realistic assessment of the situation. Embracing humor, a powerful tool for healing, re-emerges during this stage, signaling a return to a more balanced emotional state.

Stage 9: New Life

At this stage, the mourner adapts to the reality of their status and develops new friendships and connections. It demonstrates an individual's ability to triumph, overcome adversity, and build a new life.

Stage 10: Resurrection

In the final stage, true resilience prevails. The mourner finds renewed hope, strength, and a deeper, profound meaning in life. It marks the beginning of a new chapter filled with possibilities. Embracing each stage of mourning is essential in navigating the complexities of grief. It's a powerful reminder that while loss profoundly impacts us, the journey through mourning can lead to healing and transformation.

Grief and loss can often be distressing, and although each person's journey is unique, it's crucial to understand that you do not have to navigate this path

alone. You are not alone in your experiences. Regardless of the reason for your grief and loss, transition takes place. There's a release or emancipation from the circumstance or situation. Secondly, it requires a readjustment or readaptation to a new lifestyle. However, remember that it also fosters the development and renewal of relationships. Some individuals, however, become stuck for years and struggle to move forward. While I have highlighted principles related to grief as it relates to the transition of a loved one, any loss can cause one to experience these same emotions and feelings. However, there is always potential for growth, healing, and renewal after experiencing grief.

In Jewish tradition, there is a 30-day mourning period called "Sheloshim."[vi] This practice is recorded in the Old Testament and highlights how God's chosen people mourned Aaron (Num 20:29), Moses (Deut. 34:8), and Samuel (1 Sam. 25:1) for 30 days. This
mourning period begins after the funeral and typically involves an avoidance of social activities and entertainment. In fact, Jewish mourning rituals follow a specific timeline: seven days, thirty days, a year, and an annual day of remembrance.[vii]

This timeline is intended to allow the individual to gradually transition back to a normal life after an intense grieving period.[viii] The purpose is to avoid perpetual excessive grieving and mourning.[ix] No sequence of steps progresses forward in a straight line from one stage to the next, with a clear beginning and end. It is a very complex and winding journey.

Grief, bereavement, and mourning will vary depending on one's culture, personality, and tradition. Grief can be a lifelong process as you continue to adjust. While I do not intend to be insensitive or prescriptive, I believe God laid out a thoughtful framework that helps us navigate these transitions while adapting to change in a healthy fashion.

Best Practices

This devotional aims to help you move forward and "become" unstuck by applying the biblical principles that anchored me during these unexpected storms, alongside practical tools for overcoming grief and loss. Some best practices for navigating this journey include:[x]

- Keeping a journal
- Engaging in Prayer
- Getting adequate rest
- Avoiding drugs and alcohol
- Eating a balanced, nutritious diet

- Prioritizing physical activity like walking
- Consider returning to or starting school
- Seeking professional counseling as needed
- Socializing with friends and family members
- Engaging in storytelling that allows you to reminisce
- Taking up a new hobby (biking, knitting, crocheting, etc.)
- Becoming active in church or volunteering in the community and
- Avoid making major life decisions within five (5) years of a significant loss.

While not an exhaustive list, these practices help maintain emotional and physical health. The goal is to avoid complicated grief, which can make life's daily activities challenging and manifest through unhealthy behaviors such as substance abuse, withdrawal, or excessive weight loss. Engaging in these best practices can promote resilience and hope during the mourning period.

The Value of Preparation

As I mentioned earlier, my husband and parents transitioned unexpectedly. During this period, I learned the value of preparation. Unfortunately, death is guaranteed for everyone; therefore, it is imperative to

set your house in order (IS. 38:1). It is vital and essential to prepare in advance because it prevents a significant amount of stress, pressure, anxiety, hardship, difficulty, and suffering long after your loved one has transitioned. Here are some valuable suggestions I learned the hard way:

1. **Bank Account Information.** Consider adding a family member or other trusted individual to your bank accounts. Typically, you will need their name and Social Security number, which is critical for granting them access to funds following your transition.

2. **Make a Will (Last Will & Testament), Financial Power of Attorney (FPOA), and Trust.**[xi]

   - A will becomes effective after you die and outlines how your assets will be distributed following your death.
   - An FPOA allows a designated individual to make decisions on your behalf.
   - A trust allows a trustee to manage your assets for your chosen beneficiaries.

3. **Obtain several death certificate copies.** Insurance companies, banks, courts, attorneys, etc., require proof of the individual's passing. It

gives you the authority to address matters and act on their behalf.

4. **Create a living will and a durable power of attorney.**[xii] A living will helps doctors and nurses decide about life-prolonging healthcare treatments if you are unable to make decisions about your affairs due to a physical or mental condition (e.g., Alzheimer's and Dementia). Typically, when there is no hope of recovery, the presence of a terminal illness, or a permanent vegetative state, a durable power of attorney allows a designated family member or other trusted individual to make decisions on your behalf regarding your medical treatment.

Once you have completed these documents, please share them with your family members, primary care doctor, and the hospital medical record department you typically visit. Finally, an attorney is not required to complete these documents. There are currently several free sources available on the internet for use. Here is the link from the Maryland Attorney General's Website:[xiii]

https://www.marylandattorneygeneral.gov/Pages/HealthPolicy/AdvanceDirectives.aspx

5. **Organ donation.** If you wish to donate your organs or tissues, please be sure to communicate this to your family members to avoid any surprises.

6. **Purchase life insurance.** Life insurance is essential for covering funeral expenses, medical bills, mortgages, car payments, and other expenses that arise. Ensure that you name a family member or other trusted individual as the beneficiary.

7. **Purchase a funeral plot.** Decide where you would like to be buried, and consider prepaying now for your future arrangements.

8. **Decide on a Burial or Cremation.** This decision is a deeply personal choice rooted in one's religious beliefs and values.

9. **Plan your Celebration of Life Services.**
    - Decide on the location of the Celebration of Life Services (Synagogue, Church, etc.).

- Decide on the ceremony size (large or small ceremony)
- Write that obituary, decide on the poems, songs, pictures, speakers, colors, flowers, what you will wear, the color of the outfit, how your hair will be styled, pallbearers, funeral home, etc.
- Consider whether you like a wake/reception/repast after the burial.
- Decide on how you want your body transported, whether in a horse-drawn carriage or limousine.

10. **Protection and Storage of Vital Documents.** Place all important documents and paperwork in a fireproof box. Inform family members of its existence and location, and ensure they have a key or access to the key as well.

11. **Spiritual Preparation.**[xiv] Everyone dies once; this is known as physical death, in which we cease to exist on the earth. It represents the separation of the soul and spirit from the body. Every man has a sinful nature acquired from Adam, who sinned in the garden by eating the forbidden fruit and rebelling against God. When Adam experienced spiritual death, which is separation

from God, his actions impacted all of humanity, and we inherited that sinful nature.

Jesus paid the price on the cross so man would not have to experience spiritual death or separation from God. To avoid spiritual death, man must confess Jesus Christ as Lord and Savior. Failure to confess Jesus Christ would result in eternal death, which is to be eternally separated from God and experience suffering in the Lake of Fire. Affirm your faith in Jesus by confessing Him as your Lord and Savior and embracing a transformative relationship with God. The path to spiritual life begins here. There is more joy in heaven over one lost sinner who repents and returns to God than over ninety-nine righteous ones who haven't strayed away! It is as simple as saying, "Lord, forgive me of my sins and come into my heart. I confess you as my Lord and Savior. In Jesus' name, amen."

12. **Communicate, Communicate, Communicate** about your desires and wishes, as well as the steps you have taken to address the challenges they will encounter once you are gone. Do not be intimidated by the subject of death. Embrace an eternal kingdom perspective of promotion to heaven. As Jesus said, "I am the one

who raises the dead and gives them life again. Anyone who believes in me, even though he dies like anyone else, shall live again. He is given eternal life for believing in me and shall never perish." (John 11:25-26)

13. **Take Action.** Do not leave behind any unfinished business regarding your family's future legacy. Trust me, your family will be extremely grateful for your thoughtfulness long after you are gone.

Managing Grief Triggers

No one warned me that Facebook timelines, anniversaries, holidays, and other cherished memories would emotionally trigger me. I was woefully unprepared. However, as time progressed, I did not always immediately recall dates, times, or events, but I would be triggered by others who had memories of my loved ones and would share mementos, pictures, and messages. These reminders would cause me to feel sad and depressed. reminding me that even though I have moved forward and made strides in my healing journey, I am still processing the grief. Developing strategies in advance for weddings, death anniversaries, birthdays, holidays, and other significant special days is vital as you

continue to process your recovery. Recommended strategies include the following:

Build A Support System

A strong support system is not only helpful, but also crucial in managing and maintaining your emotional well-being. It is a powerful reminder that you are not alone on this journey. We are better and stronger together.

Create New Memories

Focus on creating new memories through travel, hobbies, or other engaging activities. It is not just a distraction but a beacon of hope, a reminder that life goes on and there are still beautiful moments to be experienced.

Plan Commemorative Activities

Organizing a memorial or other tribute is not just a way to honor your loved one; it is an opportunity to feel connected, to remember, and celebrate their life in a meaningful way.

Make Time for Reflection

Set aside moments for quiet reflection. This action facilitates acceptance and helps you process your emotions in a healthy manner.

Communicate Your Needs

Be open and honest about what you need and desire when the day or event arises. Sharing your feelings and asking others to support you creates an environment where compassion, hope, and healing can flourish for everyone touched by your loved one's life.

By adopting these strategies, you can navigate the emotional landscape of grief with greater resilience and hope while honoring your loved one and embracing the beauty of life ahead.

What Not To Say – Key Phrases To Avoid

Another challenge I encountered following the passing of my husband included the well-intentioned comments people made to be comforting. My husband transitioned unexpectedly in the emergency room, and while still in the hospital bed, several individuals told me, "Don't worry, you will get married again!" This comment caused me to recoil violently. What an awful thing to say!! My husband's body was still warm and not cold. I encourage individuals to be mindful of well-intentioned comments. It causes more harm than help. Here are some comments to avoid:

1. At least statements.[xv]
    - At least (fill in the name of the person) is in a better place.
    - At least (fill in the name of the person) lived a long life.
    - At least you're still young and can get married again.
    - At least they are no longer suffering.
    - At least you can still have children.
2. Do you want to talk about it?
3. Heaven has gained an angel.
4. Time heals all wounds.
5. How are you feeling?

These comments are likened to pouring salt in a wound. Job's wife said to him, "Why do you still trust God? Why don't you curse him and die?" I believe her comments added more pain and sorrow than comfort. It's essential to maintain an eternal kingdom perspective about death and remember that we serve a God who is acquainted with our griefs and sorrows (IS 53:3).

If you must speak, use few words. Consider the following comforting statements:

1. I am so sorry for your loss.
2. I am praying for you and your family.
3. I do not know what to say right now, but I'm here for you.
4. I cannot imagine how you feel, but I am here to support you in whatever way you need.

However, silence is often the best response, especially when you are unsure of what to say. Your presence is also a tremendous comfort. For example, scripture highlights the response of Job's three friends when they learned of the great tragedy that occurred in Job's life; they tore their clothes, then sprinkled dust on their heads, and cried bitterly.

And scripture says, "So, they sat down with him on the ground seven days and seven nights, and no one spoke a word to him, for they saw that his grief was very great (Job

2:13)." Words are truly inadequate during a time of loss. Your presence, companionship, silence, and empathy are the ultimate gifts you can give.

I hope these insights from my own journey can serve as valuable guidance for you. I remind you of God's promise: "But it will be different for you who respect and worshipfully fear My name. My power to make you well again will come to you. It will be like the sun that rises to shine on you. The Sun of Righteousness, a symbol of God's healing and restoring power, will arise with healing in His wings, and you shall go forth. When that happens, you will be very happy. You will jump up and down and leap for joy like young cows released from the stall when someone lets them go free (Malachi 4:2)."

Be blessed!

Let us pray

Most gracious and heavenly Father, I pray for everyone reading this devotional. I pray that they may experience a deep and profound revelation of your unwavering love—a covenant of love that cannot be shaken, regardless of the circumstances they encounter in life. I pray that Your lovingkindness will not be removed from them nor Your covenant of peace shaken. May Your loving kindness be a constant in their lives, anchoring them in a covenant of peace that no circumstance can disrupt.

Father, rescue them from the snares of the enemy of depression, hopelessness, despair, and dejection. Protect them like a bird protecting their young. Cover them with Your feathers and under Your mighty wings. With your faithfulness, form a shield around them, a rock-solid wall of protection. Lord, You are a good God, a hiding place in tough times, a strength, and a stronghold. Set them high above trouble when they call to you. Eternal God, draw and revive them in their pain. Heal the wounds of every shattered heart. Lord, have compassion upon them in their sorrow, weeping, grief, mourning, sadness, distress, unhappiness, and regrets. You are the stream of living water. Anyone who believes in You can cleave to, trust in, and rely on You and shall

flow continuously with springs and rivers of living water from their innermost being. Nourish and sustain them, Lord, in that quiet place so that times of refreshing may come from Your presence that even though they may walk through the darkest valley, they need not fear evil, for You are with them, and Your rod and Your staff will comfort them.

Remind them that Your word is a lamp to their feet and a light for their path. Even as they face hardships and difficult circumstances that make their souls faint, help them to find hope, courage, and strength in Your word. Fill their souls with Your Spirit so that they may experience the width, length, depth, and height of Your love for them and become rooted and grounded in it so they can live full lives, full in the fullness of God.

You are their hiding place and their shield. Uphold them according to Your word so they may truly live and not be ashamed. Make Your face shine upon them and guide them toward a peace-filled life. Continue to shepherd them as they navigate these challenging times. Bestow upon them Your eternal blessings and give them the joy of Your presence that lasts forever. In Jesus' name, I pray. Amen.

Table 1: Key Definitions

Loss refers to the departure of something or someone of value, such as a role, status, job, money, function, health, home, friends, family, pets, and life.

Grief is how one responds to loss either emotionally, physiologically, cognitively or behaviorally.

Key Definitions

Bereavement refers to the transition (loss) experienced due to death

Mourning is a cultural response to grief, such as celebration of life services, wakes, planting trees, etc.

Five Stages of Grief

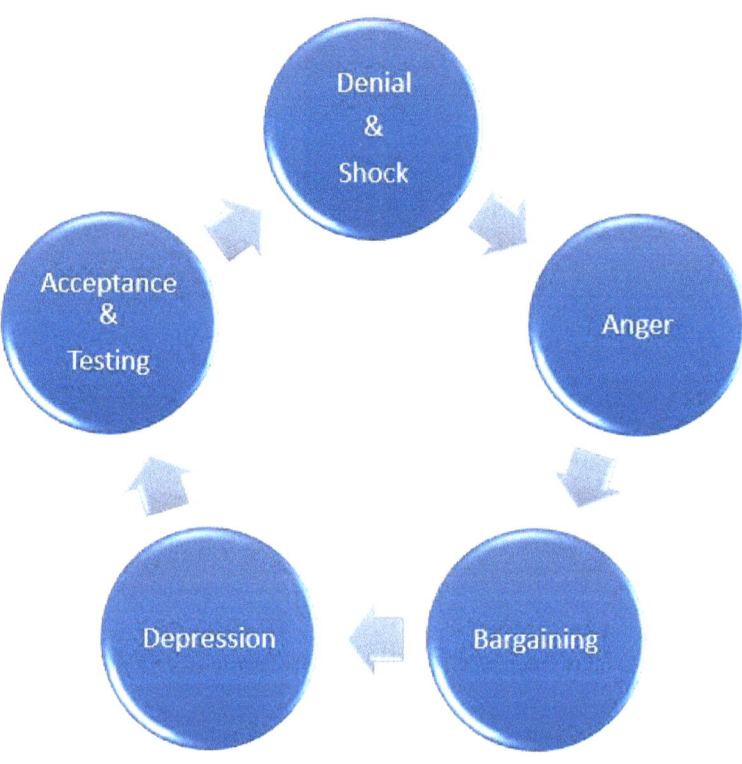

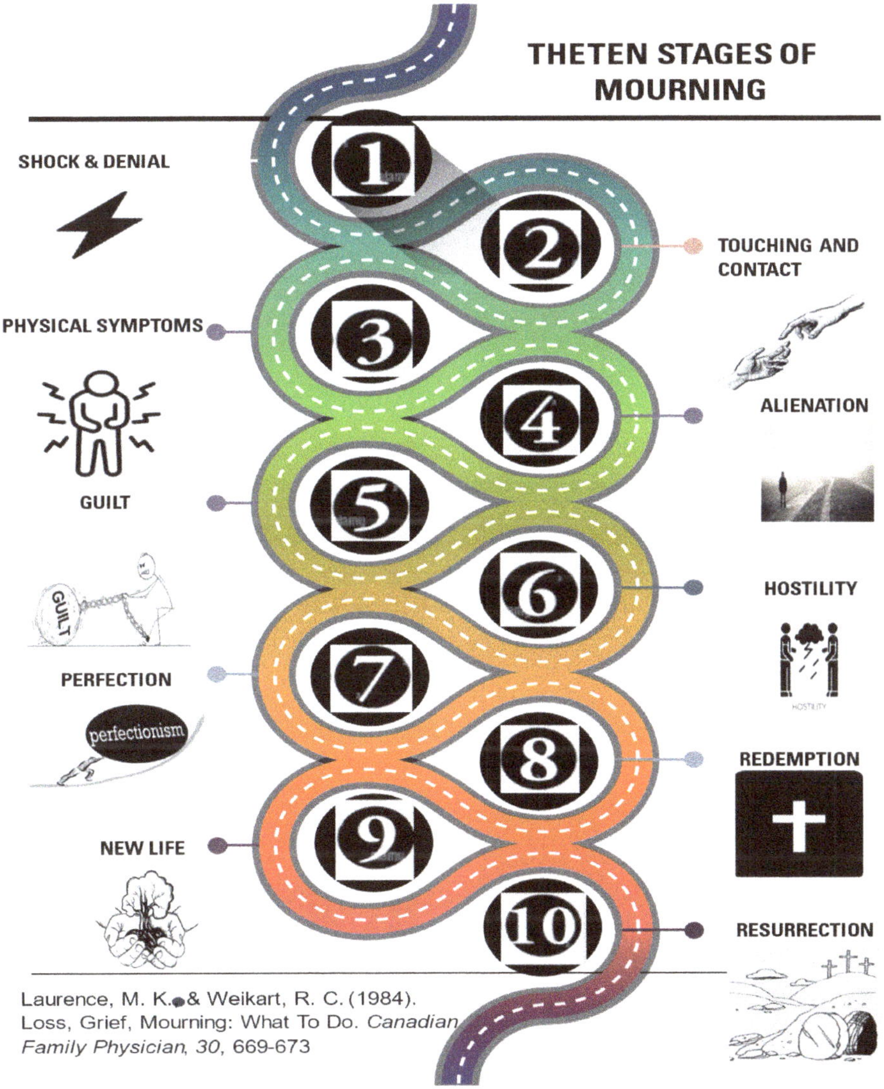

THE TEN STAGES OF MOURNING

1. SHOCK & DENIAL
2. TOUCHING AND CONTACT
3. PHYSICAL SYMPTOMS
4. ALIENATION
5. GUILT
6. HOSTILITY
7. PERFECTION
8. REDEMPTION
9. NEW LIFE
10. RESURRECTION

Laurence, M. K. & Weikart, R. C. (1984). Loss, Grief, Mourning: What To Do. *Canadian Family Physician*, 30, 669-673

Day 1

Crucial Transformation

I will bless you with a future filled with hope—a future of success, not of suffering. Jeremiah 29:11 CEV

I feel so numb right now, completely paralyzed. I don't know whether to cry or scream. I feel completely overwhelmed.

Don't be conflicted! Your life is just as valuable as the life of your loved one who transitioned. Joy is not a distant memory; It is still available. Peace is not lost. It is still available. Hope is not a mirage; it is still available. Life is not over; It is still available. Confidently know this, your life will still flourish. A flourishing finish is still available for you.

Yes, this has been a hard place, a difficult place for you, a challenging time, but a fresh anointing, a fresh oil, awaits you as you move forward. Get up and wash your face. You have grieved long enough. It is time to turn back to me and ask for help, and I will answer your prayers. Worship me with all your heart, and I will be with you, and I will accept your worship. Do not focus on how hard or difficult it is. Call to Me, and I will answer you and show you great and mighty things which you

do not know. Your life is a precious gift, and I will refresh your spirit. I will renew your mind, and I will restore your strength.

Because you have sowed and planted in tears, you shall reap a harvest of joy. Pick up those dreams that you laid down. Come out of your depression! Come out of your sadness! Come out of your despair! And, I will bless you with a future filled to the brim and overflowing with hope—a future filled with success and not suffering. This moment signifies a crucial transformation. Embrace a new anointing for this season. Your moment of transformation is here. It awaits you and your life. It is your turnaround time. It is your turnaround season, and blessings are everywhere.

Scriptures: Jer. 29:11-14 CEV; Jer. 33:3; Psalms 126:5

TODAY'S REFLECTION

WHAT IS YOUR POSITIVE THOUGHT FOR THE DAY?

WHAT ARE YOU GRATEFUL FOR TODAY?

WHAT ARE TODAY'S GOALS?

TODAY'S REFLECTION (CON'T)

WHAT WILL YOU GIVE UP TO ACCOMPLISH YOUR GOAL(S)?

WHAT IS GOD SAYING TO YOU TODAY?

WHAT GROWTH DID YOU EXPERIENCE TODAY?

Day 2

I AM with You!

I've commanded you to be strong and brave. Don't ever be afraid or discouraged! I am the Lord your God, and I will be there to help you wherever you go.
Joshua 1:9 CEV

Lord, I am fearful.

Fear Not! Following the transition of a loved one, fear becomes an overwhelming emotion. Fear of the unknown: You ask yourself, what does the future hold for me now? How do I move on? You fear the thought of being alone: How do I start over again? I am too old to start over and get married again. Listen, I leave peace with you; My perfect peace I give to you; not as the world gives do I give to you. Do not let your heart be troubled, nor let it be afraid. Let My perfect peace calm you in every circumstance and give you the courage and strength to face every challenge.

My divine peace is 100% guaranteed. My peace will go before you and serve as an umpire. And let the peace and soul harmony that comes from Me rule and act as umpire continually in your heart, deciding and settling with finality all questions that arise in your mind. I

promise that I will go in front of you and make the crooked paths straight. Allow this confident assurance to sweep over your soul and mind, washing away any fear, uncertainty, and doubt about your future. Fear will no longer bind you. Be free from the bondage of fear.

Your faith is your strength and will help you overcome any fear. Allow My promises to become rooted in your heart and affirm My love for you. Besides, within My Word, the Bible, there are 365 "fear not" messages for every day of your life. Reach out and grasp one of those promises to help you navigate this grief journey.

Scriptures: IS 41:10; Jn 14:26-27; Col. 3:15; IS 45:2; 1 Jn. 5:14; Jm. 1:21-22;

TODAY'S REFLECTION

WHAT IS YOUR POSITIVE THOUGHT FOR THE DAY?

WHAT ARE YOU GRATEFUL FOR TODAY?

WHAT ARE TODAY'S GOALS?

TODAY'S REFLECTION (CON'T)

WHAT WILL YOU GIVE UP TO ACCOMPLISH YOUR GOAL(S)?

WHAT IS GOD SAYING TO YOU TODAY?

WHAT GROWTH DID YOU EXPERIENCE TODAY?

Day 3

Arms Wide Open and Outstretched

How long must I struggle with anguish in my soul, with sorrow in my heart every day?
Psalms 13:2

How long can sorrow last? It seems like an eternity, even though I am told this temporary situation will not always last.

Grief is a process that involves various stages. Sometimes, there is denial about the loss. At other times, there is anger at the circumstances and even anger at Me. Sometimes, you find yourself asking, "Why, God? Why me?" At other times, it is bargaining with Me to change the situation. This struggle can lead to depression and feelings of hopelessness. Finally, acceptance occurs when you realize you are going to be okay and can move forward now.

Remember, I am with you through every season of life. I am always present with you. I am Immanuel, meaning "God with us." I am invested in our relationship and have a long-term commitment to you. Indeed, I am the Lord, and I am in this place with you. I will show you the path to life, and My presence will bring you great joy when you are near Me. My presence is your greatest comfort.

Therefore, choose to rejoice because this is the day that I have made. Choose to sit at My right side and be joyful. I will help you to always be aware of My presence and find comfort in Me. Seek Me with all your strength and seek My face continually. Apart from Me, You can do nothing. You must remain vitally connected to Me, carefully building yourself up in your most holy faith by praying in the Holy Spirit. Stay right at the center of My love, keeping your arms wide open and outstretched, ready to receive the mercy of Your Master, Jesus Christ. This is the unending life, the real, true life!

Scriptures: Ps. 13:2; Gen. 28:16; Ps. 16:11; Ps. 118:24; 1 Chron. 16:11; John 15:5

TODAY'S REFLECTION

WHAT IS YOUR POSITIVE THOUGHT FOR THE DAY?

WHAT ARE YOU GRATEFUL FOR TODAY?

WHAT ARE TODAY'S GOALS?

TODAY'S REFLECTION (CON'T)

WHAT WILL YOU GIVE UP TO ACCOMPLISH YOUR GOAL(S)?

WHAT IS GOD SAYING TO YOU TODAY?

WHAT GROWTH DID YOU EXPERIENCE TODAY?

Day 4

Fight the Good Fight

All praise to the God and Father of our Master, Jesus the Messiah! Father of all mercy! God of all healing counsel! He comes alongside us when we go through hard times.
2 Corinthians 1:3

God, I don't understand. This hole in my heart will not go away. A piece of me is missing, and I am still experiencing intense sorrow. Your name is Amazing Counselor, Strong God, Eternal Father, and Prince of Wholeness. The wholeness You bring has no limits. It only has infinite value. When I come near to you, you draw near to me. I need to be near You because I need You to give me life. I remain vitally connected to You because You comfort and strengthen me so wonderfully in my hardships and trials.

You are the God who sees me. Therefore, I will experience joy because you hear my anguished cries. In times of distress, the joy of the Lord is my strength, my refuge, my stronghold, my fortress, and my hiding place. I will cultivate a mindset of joy when waves of grief threaten to wash over me. I exchange my sorrow for Your joy, which exists in heaven.

Your joy empowers me because it is dependent on Your strength, not my circumstances. Therefore, my cup overflows with joy. You are essential and indispensable to me. I will fight the good fight of faith and maintain my joy. I will endure hardship and suffering as a good soldier of Jesus Christ, knowing that I am more than a conqueror and that my faith will see me through.

Scriptures: Gen. 16:13; Neh. 8:10; Nah. 1:7; John 15:11; James 4:8; Ps. 63:1; 2 Tim. 2:3; 2 Tim. 4:7; Rom. 8:37

TODAY'S REFLECTION

WHAT IS YOUR POSITIVE THOUGHT FOR THE DAY?

WHAT ARE YOU GRATEFUL FOR TODAY?

WHAT ARE TODAY'S GOALS?

TODAY'S REFLECTION (CON'T)

WHAT WILL YOU GIVE UP TO ACCOMPLISH YOUR GOAL(S)?

WHAT IS GOD SAYING TO YOU TODAY?

WHAT GROWTH DID YOU EXPERIENCE TODAY?

Day 5

Unquenchable Joy Is My Secret Weapon

"My flesh and my heart may fail, but God is the strength of my heart and my portion forever."
Psalm 73:26

I am alone and afflicted, isolated in my loneliness. I am shrinking on the inside, and it is unbearable. I am helpless, overwhelmed, and in deep distress. Look at me and help me! Have mercy, oh Lord. I am all alone, in big trouble, and in deep distress. My heart and mind are fighting each other as my problems go from bad to worse. Call a truce to this civil war and save me. The troubles of my heart are multiplied.

But remember, Beloved, I am the Lord who saves. I save those who are crushed in spirit. I am Immanuel, the God who is with you. I am close to those whose hearts are breaking. My presence is a comfort to you, and I will heal your broken heart and bind up your wounds. When you feel joyless, I am your secret weapon, adding value to your life so you can overflow with joy.

I encourage you to cling to what is good, rejoice in hope, remain constant in prayer, contribute to the needs of the saints, and seek to show hospitality to others. Then, I will restore joy to you as you build yourself up in your

most holy faith, praying in the Holy Spirit. Building yourself up is My strategy for the faithful whose steps are ordered by the Lord. Then, I will endow you with eternal happiness and fill you with the unquenchable joy of my presence.

Scriptures: Isaiah 61:10; Ps. 34:18; Rom. 12:9-21; Jude 1:20

TODAY'S REFLECTION

WHAT IS YOUR POSITIVE THOUGHT FOR THE DAY?

WHAT ARE YOU GRATEFUL FOR TODAY?

WHAT ARE TODAY'S GOALS?

TODAY'S REFLECTION (CON'T)

WHAT WILL YOU GIVE UP TO ACCOMPLISH YOUR GOAL(S)?

WHAT IS GOD SAYING TO YOU TODAY?

WHAT GROWTH DID YOU EXPERIENCE TODAY?

Day 6

You are my Beloved!

Set me as a seal upon your heart, As a seal upon your arm;
For love is as strong as death.
Song of Solomon 8:6

I am immensely miserable and deeply sorrowful about my loss. All my days are bad, and every day is difficult. My soul is weary with sorrow and grief.

The secret to overcoming misery and sorrow is "Thank you!" Enter My gates with thanksgiving and My courts with praise. Be thankful! Praise Me, exalt Me, and bless My Name. Then My grace will become sufficient for you, for My power is made perfect in weakness. My power will rest upon you. I will be your strength, personal bravery, and invincible army; I will make your feet like hind's feet, and you will walk and not stand still in terror but walk and make spiritual progress upon your high places of trouble, suffering, and responsibility. Generosity, random acts of kindness, and good deeds will remove your suffering. Encourage yourself by pouring yourself out to the hungry, poor, and needy. This action will satisfy the desire of the afflicted, and then your light will arise in the darkness and your gloom as the noonday.

Focus on the future without dwelling on the past. Forget about the past and what happened; don't keep replaying old stories or memories. Be alert, be present. I'm about to do something brand-new. It's bursting out! Don't you see it? There it is! I'm making a road through the desert, rivers in the badlands. Write this down, for these words are trustworthy and true. This month shall mark a new beginning for you. It shall be the first month of the year for you. I will restore your joy, peace, strength, health, wealth, and passion for life. Your present troubles are minor and won't last very long. They produce glory that vastly outweighs your difficulties and will last forever! I am the Lord, your God, and your end will increase significantly. You can count on My faithfulness and commitment to you.

Scriptures: Prov. 15:15; Ps. 119:28; 2 Cor. 12:9; Hab. 3:19; Ps. 100:4; IS 58:10; Exo 12:2; IS 43:19; Job 8:7; Ps. 100:4; 1 Pet. 1:6-7; 2 Cor. 4:17; Rom. 8:18

TODAY'S REFLECTION

WHAT IS YOUR POSITIVE THOUGHT FOR THE DAY?

WHAT ARE YOU GRATEFUL FOR TODAY?

WHAT ARE TODAY'S GOALS?

TODAY'S REFLECTION (CON'T)

WHAT WILL YOU GIVE UP TO ACCOMPLISH YOUR GOAL(S)?

WHAT IS GOD SAYING TO YOU TODAY?

WHAT GROWTH DID YOU EXPERIENCE TODAY?

Day 7

Take Heart and Be Courageous

"I am with you always, even to the end of the age."
Matthew 28:20

Why do You seem so far away? Why, O LORD, do you stand far away? Why do you hide yourself in times of trouble? How long, O LORD? Will you forget me forever? How long will you hide your face from me? How long must I take counsel in my soul, having sorrow in my heart daily? Why are you slow to act on my behalf? Yet, I know You hear me, O Lord, for I am in trouble; My eye wastes away with grief, yes, my soul and my body! I am a broken vessel. Please help me overcome this feeling of hopelessness.

I know You to be a good God. Even though I walk through the darkest valley, I will fear no evil, for you are with me; Your rod and Your staff comfort me. Allow me to feel the lasting joy of Your presence because in Your presence is fullness of joy, and at Your right hand are pleasures forevermore. You are my rock of refuge, a fortress of defense to save me. Hide me in the secret place of Your presence. Blessed be the Lord, for You have shown me Your marvelous kindness and guided my steps.

When you draw near to Me, I will draw near to you. I will lift you out of the pit of despair, full of mud and mire, and set your feet on a hard, firm path. I will support you until you are steady enough and regain your strength to confidently continue the journey. Take heart and be courageous; I will strengthen you because you have chosen to hope in Me. I will shine My face on you, My servant. Then, your heart will leap in your womb for joy. Blessed are you because you believed, for there will be a fulfillment of everything that I, the Lord, promised you. You are undeniably loved, cherished, and valued by Me eternally.

Scriptures: Psalms 10:1; Psalms 13; Luke 1:44-46; Psalms 31; Jm. 4:8; Psalms 4:2

TODAY'S REFLECTION

WHAT IS YOUR POSITIVE THOUGHT FOR THE DAY?

WHAT ARE YOU GRATEFUL FOR TODAY?

WHAT ARE TODAY'S GOALS?

TODAY'S REFLECTION (CON'T)

WHAT WILL YOU GIVE UP TO ACCOMPLISH YOUR GOAL(S)?

WHAT IS GOD SAYING TO YOU TODAY?

WHAT GROWTH DID YOU EXPERIENCE TODAY?

Day 8

Be of Good Cheer. Take Courage.

And they who know Your name [who have experience and acquaintance with Your mercy] will lean on and confidently put their trust in You, for You, Lord, have not forsaken those who seek (inquire of and for) You [on the authority of God's Word and the right of their necessity].
Psalms 9:10

My God, my God, why have you forsaken me? God, I am so anguished in my soul. Why God? Why? What did I do to deserve this? Why do You hate me so much? You are supposed to be in control! Why didn't you stop it? Why did you allow it to happen? Not a day goes by when I'm not overcome with anger or a sense of abandonment. Why have you brought this trouble on your servant? What have I done to displease you?

Do you really believe that I have abandoned you? Consider this. People sell two birds for just one small coin. But I take care of these little birds. None can fall to the ground and die without Me knowing it. I even know how many hairs there are on your head. You are more valuable and precious to Me than many little birds. I have told you these things so that you may have

[perfect] peace and confidence in Me. You will have tribulation, trials, distress, and frustration in the world, but be of good cheer [take courage; be confident, certain, undaunted]!

I have overcome the world. I have deprived it of power to harm you and have conquered it for you. While I understand your grief, refuse to let resentment and bitterness take root in your heart. When you call to Me, I will heal you. I will comfort, console, and encourage you in every trouble, calamity, and affliction you face. So that you may also be able to comfort, console, and encourage those in any trouble or distress, sharing the same hope and strength that I offer you.

Scriptures: Psalms 22:1; John 16:33; Numbers 11:11; Matthew 10:29-31; Psalms 30:2; 2 Corinthians 1:3-5

TODAY'S REFLECTION

WHAT IS YOUR POSITIVE THOUGHT FOR THE DAY?

WHAT ARE YOU GRATEFUL FOR TODAY?

WHAT ARE TODAY'S GOALS?

TODAY'S REFLECTION (CON'T)

WHAT WILL YOU GIVE UP TO ACCOMPLISH YOUR GOAL(S)?

WHAT IS GOD SAYING TO YOU TODAY?

WHAT GROWTH DID YOU EXPERIENCE TODAY?

Day 9

Walk Boldly Like a Lion

To all who mourn in Israel, He will give a crown of beauty for ashes, a joyous blessing instead of mourning, festive praise instead of despair.
Isaiah 61:3-4 NLT

How will I survive without them, Lord? I am all alone. So many dreams and so many plans.

Be convinced and confident of this very thing: I have begun a good work in you and will continue to perfect and complete it. I will equip you with everything necessary to perform my will, which is the path I have set for you to fulfill your purpose. Don't miss Me at this moment in this season.

Find My words, meditate on them, and they will sustain you. They are food for your hungry soul. They bring joy and rejoicing to your sorrowing heart. I will turn your circumstances around, transforming your challenges into opportunities for growth and blessings. I am not finished with you yet.

Listen to My voice guiding you, saying, "This is the way; walk here." I will establish your steps. Trust in Me with all your heart and lean not to your own understanding; in

all your ways submit to Me, and I will make your paths straight. My commandments are clear, offering insight into living and providing a reward for those who obey them.

Remember, I will never leave you nor forsake you. I have never forsaken the righteous or their children. I will bless you with abundant provisions. So do not be anxious about tomorrow. I will take care of your tomorrow too. Live one day at a time. Give your entire attention to what I am doing right now, and do not get worked up or anxious about what may or may not happen. I will help you deal with whatever challenges arise when the time comes. I have given you my word. Now, be as bold as a lion.

Scriptures: 2 Pet. 1:3; Heb. 13:5; Ps. 37:5; Ps. 132:15; Prov. 16:9; Phil. 2:13; Heb. 13:21

TODAY'S REFLECTION

WHAT IS YOUR POSITIVE THOUGHT FOR THE DAY?

WHAT ARE YOU GRATEFUL FOR TODAY?

WHAT ARE TODAY'S GOALS?

TODAY'S REFLECTION (CON'T)

WHAT WILL YOU GIVE UP TO ACCOMPLISH YOUR GOAL(S)?

WHAT IS GOD SAYING TO YOU TODAY?

WHAT GROWTH DID YOU EXPERIENCE TODAY?

Day 10

Calming the Storm

The Lord is near to the brokenhearted and saves the crushed in spirit.
Psalms 34:18

I am weary and burdened with grief and deep sorrow. Lord, I cry out to You; make haste to help me. My soul melts from heaviness. Strengthen me according to Your word.

My child, I will be there with you when you are in over your head and feel overwhelmed. When you are in rough waters, you will not go down. It will not be a dead end when you are between a rock and a hard place because I am your personal God, The Holy One of Israel, your Savior. I paid a huge price for you. You mean so much to me. I will heal the wounds of your shattered heart. I am near to all who call upon me. I uphold all who stumble and raise up all who are bowed down. Keep your tongue from speaking evil and negativity. Set a guard over your mouth and a watch over the door of your lips. Remember, I am always with you, especially in times of distress, offering my presence and comfort.

What you sow in tears, you shall reap in joy. As you journey forward, even while weeping, you shall bear seeds of hope for sowing and shall doubtlessly experience overwhelming joy again. This transformation from sorrow to joy is a testament to the hope and optimism that I bring into your life. When you cry out to me in your trouble, I will bring you out of all your distress. I will calm the storm so that the waves are still.

Cast the whole of your care, anxieties, worries, concerns, and burdens once and for all upon Me because I care for you affectionately and care about you watchfully. Let My peace, the inner calm you receive from walking with Me daily, be the deciding factor in your heart, addressing questions, doubts, and fears that arise. I give power, strength, and vitality to the faint and weary. Pile your troubles upon My shoulders, release the weight of it, and I will carry the load and help you out. This act of sharing your burdens with Me will bring you relief and comfort, knowing that you are not alone in your struggles. So, you can increase your strength without slipping, failing, or falling.

Scriptures. IS 43:1-4; PS 147:3; PS 145:18; PS 141:1; PS 141:3; PS 126:5-6; PS 119; 28; PS 107:29; IS 40:29; PS 55:22

TODAY'S REFLECTION

WHAT IS YOUR POSITIVE THOUGHT FOR THE DAY?

WHAT ARE YOU GRATEFUL FOR TODAY?

WHAT ARE TODAY'S GOALS?

TODAY'S REFLECTION (CON'T)

WHAT WILL YOU GIVE UP TO ACCOMPLISH YOUR GOAL(S)?

WHAT IS GOD SAYING TO YOU TODAY?

WHAT GROWTH DID YOU EXPERIENCE TODAY?

Day 11

A New Season Is On The Horizon

To everything, there is a season. A time for every purpose under heaven.
Ecclesiastes 3:1

Lord, it has been years, and I still feel stuck. I spend time questioning the past and worrying about the future. I look back on my past life and ponder the future.

Remember, I, the Lord, have a perfect timing for everything. I am the author and finisher of your faith. I will transform your life and guide you forward because I hold the entire roadmap of your life. I want you to complete what I initiated in your life. A new season is on the horizon. Trust in my purpose for your life. I will open and close doors as needed. Just stay attuned to My voice.

Here's what I want you to do with My guidance. Offer your everyday, ordinary life—sleeping, eating, working, and living—as a gift to Me. Trusting me to do what I can for you is your best decision. Keep your focus on Me. Don't lose heart, but follow the example of those who, through faith and patience, inherited what I promised. Listen, do not delay. Be like those who

persevered with unwavering faith and received everything promised.

I am sharing these words with you so you understand the urgency of the moment. I seek someone with a heart like Mine. You will face challenges ahead. But do not be afraid; they are of little significance. What matters most to Me is that you complete what I have entrusted to you. The Holy Spirit, your Helper, will make everything clear to you. And I will remind you of all I have shared with you. Cast off every burden and run the race set before you with endurance. You can accomplish all things through Me. I will dwell within you, and I will fortify you. My divine presence will lead you in the right direction. I, the Lord, make everything beautiful in its time. This is your *Kairos* moment. Your season of preparation is over. Let us move forward together!

Scripture: Ecc. 3:11; Heb. 11:2; Acts 20:24; Rom. 12:2; 1 Cor. 9:24; Heb. 6:12; 1 Sam. 13:14; Heb. 12:1; Gal 2:20

TODAY'S REFLECTION

WHAT IS YOUR POSITIVE THOUGHT FOR THE DAY?

WHAT ARE YOU GRATEFUL FOR TODAY?

WHAT ARE TODAY'S GOALS?

TODAY'S REFLECTION (CON'T)

WHAT WILL YOU GIVE UP TO ACCOMPLISH YOUR GOAL(S)?

WHAT IS GOD SAYING TO YOU TODAY?

WHAT GROWTH DID YOU EXPERIENCE TODAY?

Day 12

Peace is your inheritance

**My peace is the legacy I leave to you. I don't give gifts like those of this world. Do not let your heart be troubled or fearful.
John 14:27**

Will I ever recover from this loss? Will I ever feel better?

There is no comparison between the present hard times and the brighter days ahead. I will wipe away every tear from your eyes, for a time will come when you shall laugh with joy again! Joy is on the way. It is coming in the morning. Even when your flesh and heart fail, I will strengthen your heart. My eyes roam throughout the earth, seeking to support those whose hearts are completely devoted to Me. But you asked Me for help, and I will give you the victory. I am constantly looking for people who are committed to Me. Remember, I am always with you; My divine presence is your constant source of hope, comfort, and support.

No challenge or hardship that comes your way, is beyond what others have faced. All you need to remember is that you are not alone. I will never let you

down. I will never push you past your limits. I will always be there to help you get through it. I am a faithful God to My Word, and I have a compassionate nature. You can trust Me not to let you be tried and tested beyond your ability, strength, or endurance. I will always provide a way of escape, a landing place that you may be strong enough to bear up under it and endure patiently.

Do not let your heart be troubled. Do not be anxious for anything. Instead of worrying, pray. Let petitions and praises shape your worries into prayers. Share your concerns and burdens with Me, and before you know it, you will experience My wholeness, and everything will come together for good. Do not be afraid, have faith. You will regain all that you have lost and recover all. Embrace hope for restoration. I will surely restore everything you lost, and I will come and pick up all the scattered pieces of your life with compassion.

Scriptures: Rom. 8:18; Rev. 21:4; PS 73:26; Luke 6:21; 2 Chron. 16:9; 1 Cor. 10:13; John 14:1; Phil 4:6; Mark 5:36; Deut. 30:3

TODAY'S REFLECTION

WHAT IS YOUR POSITIVE THOUGHT FOR THE DAY?

WHAT ARE YOU GRATEFUL FOR TODAY?

WHAT ARE TODAY'S GOALS?

TODAY'S REFLECTION (CON'T)

WHAT WILL YOU GIVE UP TO ACCOMPLISH YOUR GOAL(S)?

WHAT IS GOD SAYING TO YOU TODAY?

WHAT GROWTH DID YOU EXPERIENCE TODAY?

Day 13

Finding the Silver Lining

"I will bless the Lord at all times; his praise shall continually be in my mouth." Psalms 34:1

How do I find the silver lining in all this? Despite the overwhelming darkness, I stand my ground, God, shouting for help. Each morning, I pray on my knees at daybreak. I question, God, why do you seem distant? For as long as I can remember, I have been hurting; I have taken the worst you can hand out, and I have had enough. Loss has blazed through my life; I'm bleeding, black-and-blue. I have been attacked fiercely on every side, with blows raining down till I am nearly dead. The only friend I have left is Darkness. I feel defeated, but I refuse to surrender and give up.

I will come before your presence with thanksgiving. I will enter your courts with praise. I will joyfully sing to You with psalms. The Lord, the supreme ruler, is a great God and a great King above all gods. I kneel down and worship before the Lord, my maker, and my God. I belong to your flock, hear Your voice, and choose not to harden my heart. I have set my love upon You, and I trust in Your promises. You will deliver me. You will anoint my head with fresh oil, establish me with Your right hand, and fill my horn. Your covenant with me is unbreakable. I shall flourish like a palm tree planted in the house of the Lord who is rooted and

grounded. You are my rock and my anchor. In the multitude of my anxieties within me, Your comfort delights my soul with joy. I open my eyes to the future, and I will sing praises to the Lord! I will shout joyfully to the rock of my salvation.

My soul longs for Your salvation, and I hope in Your word. You are my hiding place and my shield. Do not let my hope lead to shame. Hold me up, and I shall be safe. My help comes from the Lord. I trust in Your ability to preserve my soul. Make your face shine upon your servant.

"For the time to favor you has arrived. Yes, your set-appointed time has come. I will increase you more and more. I will save you and grant you prosperity now. This is my doing, and it's marvelous and wonderous in my eyes," thus says the Lord.

Scriptures: Ps. 89: 17-22; Ps 91:15; Ps. 92 10-15; Ps. 94:19; Ps. 95: 1-9; Ps. 100:4; Ps. 114: 15; Ps. 118:23-25; Ps. 119:81,116,135

TODAY'S REFLECTION

WHAT IS YOUR POSITIVE THOUGHT FOR THE DAY?

WHAT ARE YOU GRATEFUL FOR TODAY?

WHAT ARE TODAY'S GOALS?

TODAY'S REFLECTION (CON'T)

WHAT WILL YOU GIVE UP TO ACCOMPLISH YOUR GOAL(S)?

WHAT IS GOD SAYING TO YOU TODAY?

WHAT GROWTH DID YOU EXPERIENCE TODAY?

Day 14

Focus on What Truly Counts

Now, may the Lord of peace himself give you peace at all times and in every way. The Lord be with all of you. 2 Thess. 3:16

Did I miss something, Lord? Could I have prevented this from happening? The guilt I feel is more than I can handle; I feel crushed beneath its weight. This heavy burden is too much for me. I am collapsing under an avalanche of guilt and remorse.

Do not dwell on the coulda, shoulda, and woulda. Remember, it is appointed unto men once to die. This is an inevitable truth, regardless of your wealth, race, or status. It is the destiny of every individual. The living should take this to heart, learn to number their days, and gain a heart of wisdom. Let Me teach you how to live wisely and well with purpose and clarity! Prioritize expressing your feelings and love on a regular basis. Make forgiveness a habit to avoid the pain of regret and guilt when transitions occur.

Spend quality time with those you love and care about. Do not pursue the things of this world that take you away from your family: fame, power, position, promotion, social status, status symbols, and wealth. Cease from the

busyness of life and re-evaluate your priorities. Travel and explore the world, this beautiful planet that I created. Do not hold onto anger; instead, be kind to others. Laughter is beneficial for the soul, so make a point to find reasons to laugh often. Serve Me wholeheartedly and always seek the best in every situation. Do not look back; keep moving forward by focusing on what lies ahead. If you do these things, you can build a life free from regret and guilt.

My purpose is to give life in all its fullness. I came so that You may have and enjoy life and have it in abundance, to the full, till it overflows. Do not dwell on the past. Press on. Leave the old life behind and put everything on the line for this mission, this new life. Sprint toward the only goal that counts: to cross the line, to win the prize, and to hear God's call to resurrection life found exclusively in Me, the Anointed One. Rest assured, and live with good cheer, knowing that any believer who dies in Me is away from the earthly body and at home with Me.

Scriptures: 2 Cor. 5:6-8; Phil. 3:13-14; Jn. 10:10; Ps. 90:12; Ecc. 7:2; Heb. 9:27; Ps. 38:4

TODAY'S REFLECTION

WHAT IS YOUR POSITIVE THOUGHT FOR THE DAY?

WHAT ARE YOU GRATEFUL FOR TODAY?

WHAT ARE TODAY'S GOALS?

TODAY'S REFLECTION (CON'T)

WHAT WILL YOU GIVE UP TO ACCOMPLISH YOUR GOAL(S)?

WHAT IS GOD SAYING TO YOU TODAY?

WHAT GROWTH DID YOU EXPERIENCE TODAY?

Day 15

I PRESS ON

For everything that happens in life—there is a season, a right time for everything under heaven. Ecclesiastes 3: 1

How do I say goodbye when I do not want to? How do I let go?

Beloved, do not grieve like people who have no hope. When Jesus returns, He will bring back those believers who have died in faith. This is not a farewell but a 'see you later.' Now is your time of grief, but you will see them again, rejoice, and no one will take away your joy. I will wipe every tear from your eyes. There will be no more death or mourning or crying or pain. Remember, I am your source of strength in times of trouble, always ready to help in times of need.

Move forward and embrace the journey ahead. Fear not; stand still, firm, confident, and undismayed, seeing the salvation of the Lord. I will make My face shine upon you, and you will put My glory on display. What the devil meant for evil, I will turn it around for good. Be strong and courageous; do not fear nor be afraid, for I am the

LORD your God, the One who goes with you. I will not leave you nor forsake you. My divine plan for you is to prosper you and not harm you, a plan to give you hope and a future. This plan is your purpose, your hope, and your future.

I will order your footsteps and make every crooked path straight when you face challenges at work, decisions in relationships, or uncertainties in your health. Because I delight in every detail of your life, you will never fall or fail. I will teach you how to live right and well. I will show you what to do and where to go. Rise in a new authority. Walk in victory confidently, knowing that I will turn it around. Remain confident that you will see the goodness of the Lord in the land of the living.

Scriptures: Gen. 50:30; Exo 14:13-16; Deut. 31:6; Ps. 37:23; Psalm 37:23-24; Isaiah 48:17; IS 40:31

TODAY'S REFLECTION

WHAT IS YOUR POSITIVE THOUGHT FOR THE DAY?

WHAT ARE YOU GRATEFUL FOR TODAY?

WHAT ARE TODAY'S GOALS?

TODAY'S REFLECTION (CON'T)

WHAT WILL YOU GIVE UP TO ACCOMPLISH YOUR GOAL(S)?

WHAT IS GOD SAYING TO YOU TODAY?

WHAT GROWTH DID YOU EXPERIENCE TODAY?

Day 16

Refocus

**I look behind me, and you're there, then up ahead, and you're there, too—your reassuring presence, coming and going. This is too much, too wonderful—
I can't take it all in! Psalm 139:5-6**

No one understands the anguish of my heart. O Lord, I cry from the depths of despair for your help: "Hear me! Answer! Help me!"

Cast all your anxieties and anguish upon Me, for I care for you and will relieve you of all your anguish. I am near to the brokenhearted and save the crushed in spirit. I promise to heal you, restore you, and grant you prosperity and lasting peace. Trust in this promise, and you will find comfort and hope in the face of your pain and loss. Fill your mind by meditating on things true, noble, reputable, authentic, compelling, gracious—the best, not the worst; the beautiful, not the ugly; things to praise, not things to curse. Put what you learned from Me into practice, and I will make everything work together.

Remember, you will reunite with your loved ones again, your heart will overflow with joy, and no one will take

your joy away. I will heal you, restore you, and give you prosperity and lasting peace. I will reestablish you better than before. I will cleanse you of all the guilt, sorrow, and heartache. You will think of your loved one forgiving you as well. And you will experience deep-seated joy. When others hear of all the joy and peace bestowed upon you, they will marvel at the goodness of God.

Embrace every promise I have preordained for you with boldness. As you trust in Me, you will discover a new strength and renew your power. You will be as strong as eagles, soaring to new heights. You will walk and run without growing weary. When your heart is entwined with Mine, you will experience divine strength. You will navigate life without giving up - never winded, never weary, never tired, never faint. This is the promise I make to you, My beloved, to empower you and instill resilience in you, even in the face of life's most daunting challenges.

Scriptures: PS 130:1-2; Jer. 33:6-9; 1 Pet. 5:7; Ps. 34:18; Phil. 4:8

TODAY'S REFLECTION

WHAT IS YOUR POSITIVE THOUGHT FOR THE DAY?

WHAT ARE YOU GRATEFUL FOR TODAY?

WHAT ARE TODAY'S GOALS?

TODAY'S REFLECTION (CON'T)

WHAT WILL YOU GIVE UP TO ACCOMPLISH YOUR GOAL(S)?

WHAT IS GOD SAYING TO YOU TODAY?

WHAT GROWTH DID YOU EXPERIENCE TODAY?

Day 17

The Fountain of Life

He nurses them when they are sick and soothes their pains and worries. PS. 41:3

Lord, I'm feeling overwhelmed and exhausted. What's wrong with me? I'm at a loss for words, my voice fading as I sigh. Every day seems to end in the same place—lying in bed, covered in tears, my pillow wet with sorrow.

Where are you, my child? Who told you that something was wrong with you? You are not just special to Me; you are chosen, precious, and honored in My sight, and I love you. I have chosen you. Do not be afraid; I have redeemed you. I have called your name. You are mine. When you are in over your head, I will be there with you. When you are in rough waters, you will not go down. It will not be a dead end when you are between a rock and a hard place. I am your hiding place from every storm of life. I even keep you from getting into trouble! I will surround you with songs of victory.

Though the deepest pains may linger through the night, joy greets the soul with the smile of the morning. You will grieve, but that grief will give birth to great joy. In My presence is fullness of joy. At My right hand are

pleasures forevermore. I will instruct you in the night season, guiding you through the darkness and the challenges, and remain at your right hand. Be firmly convinced that nothing—nothing living or dead, angelic or demonic, today or tomorrow, high or low, thinkable or unthinkable—absolutely *nothing* can get between us.

Let none of this faze you because I love you. No matter what comes, you will always taste victory through and with Me. In all things, you are more than a conqueror. You are the apple of My eye, and I will hide you under the shadow of My wings. Do not lose heart. Only believe, and you will see the goodness of the Lord while you are alive. Wait on me; be strong and courageous, and I will strengthen your heart. I am your strength, your shield, and a present help in trouble. Therefore, let your heart greatly rejoice and praise Me because I preserve the faithful.

Scriptures: Rom. 8:37-39; Ps. 32:7; IS 43:4; IS 43:10; PS 30:5; John 16:20; PS 16:7-11; PS 17:8; PS. 31:23.

TODAY'S REFLECTION

WHAT IS YOUR POSITIVE THOUGHT FOR THE DAY?

WHAT ARE YOU GRATEFUL FOR TODAY?

WHAT ARE TODAY'S GOALS?

TODAY'S REFLECTION (CON'T)

WHAT WILL YOU GIVE UP TO ACCOMPLISH YOUR GOAL(S)?

WHAT IS GOD SAYING TO YOU TODAY?

WHAT GROWTH DID YOU EXPERIENCE TODAY?

Day 18

Crisis of Faith

**My flesh and my heart fail, but God is the strength of my heart and my portion forever.
Psalms 73:26**

God, I have a crisis of faith. I prayed, fasted, and called the church elders, yet I experienced profound loss. This situation is impacting my faith. Yet, I believe. Help me with my unbelief.

Seek Me, and you will find Me when you seek Me with all your heart. You need perfected faith. Difficult circumstances may cause you to forget everything I have done, leading to doubts about who I am. Do not run from tests and hardships. As difficult as they are, you will ultimately find joy in them; if you embrace them, your faith will blossom under pressure and teach you true patience as you endure. True patience brought on by endurance will equip you to complete the long journey and cross the finish line—mature, complete, and lacking nothing. Remember, it is in seeking Me that you will find the strength and guidance to persevere.

Remember, I am the source of all hope, ready to infuse your life with abundant joy and peace even amid your faith crisis so that your hope will overflow through the power of the Holy Spirit. Keep your eyes on Jesus, My son, who both began and finished this race we are in. Study how He did it. Because He never lost sight of where He was headed—that exhilarating finish with God—enabled Him to endure the cross, shame, and everything else. His unwavering focus on the ultimate goal enabled Him to endure all hardships. When you find your faith waning, go over that story, item by item, and remember the hostility He plowed through. This will shoot adrenaline into your soul, fuel your faith, and ignite a fire within your soul.

Scriptures: Jer. 29:12; Mark 9:24; Rom. 15:24; Jm. 1:2-4

TODAY'S REFLECTION

WHAT IS YOUR POSITIVE THOUGHT FOR THE DAY?

WHAT ARE YOU GRATEFUL FOR TODAY?

WHAT ARE TODAY'S GOALS?

TODAY'S REFLECTION (CON'T)

WHAT WILL YOU GIVE UP TO ACCOMPLISH YOUR GOAL(S)?

WHAT IS GOD SAYING TO YOU TODAY?

WHAT GROWTH DID YOU EXPERIENCE TODAY?

Day 19

Beyond What You Can Ask or Think

Instead of shame and dishonor, you shall have a double portion of prosperity and everlasting joy.

Isaiah 61:7

Lord, I need help and am embarrassed to ask others for assistance.

I am a very present help in trouble. Lift up your eyes. Your help comes from Me, the Lord. I am the God of the Breakthroughs and the Way Maker. I will rescue those who call out to Me for help and those who have no one to help them. I will help and protect the lives of people in need.

Trust in me; do not be afraid because I am your strength and song. I will give you unyielding and impenetrable strength, empowering you in your journey. I delight in every detail of your life and cherish every step that you take. You will never stumble or fall because I hold your hand securely. Your life is in My hands. I will teach you how to live right and well. I will show you what to do and where to go. Seek Me in all you do, and I will show you which path to take.

I will adorn you with a beautiful crown in exchange for your ashes. I will anoint you with gladness instead of sorrow and wrap you in victory, joy, and praise instead of depression and sadness. And you shall be magnificent, like great towering oak trees, planted, strong, and graceful, bringing Me glory. I will give you double for your trouble. I have already gone ahead of you, making every crooked path straight.

When I decree a thing, it shall be established. Commit to Me whatever you do, and your plans shall prosper and succeed. I will bless the latter part of your life more than the former part. Keep a firm grip on your faith. Remember, this suffering is but a fleeting moment in the grand scheme of eternity. I am a kind and generous God who has great plans for you. I will personally come and lift you up, restore you, support you, strengthen you, and ground you. I will firmly establish you in place and make you stronger than ever. Never forget that I am always guiding you every step of the way.

Scriptures: Prov. 16:3; Ps. 29:11; IS 12:2; PS 59:16-17; PS 37:23-24; PS 31:14-15; IS 48:17; Prov. 3:16; PS 121; Job 42:12; 1 Pet. 5:10-11; PS 72:12-13

TODAY'S REFLECTION

WHAT IS YOUR POSITIVE THOUGHT FOR THE DAY?

WHAT ARE YOU GRATEFUL FOR TODAY?

WHAT ARE TODAY'S GOALS?

TODAY'S REFLECTION (CON'T)

WHAT WILL YOU GIVE UP TO ACCOMPLISH YOUR GOAL(S)?

WHAT IS GOD SAYING TO YOU TODAY?

WHAT GROWTH DID YOU EXPERIENCE TODAY?

Day 20

Don't Hesitate

Go your way; as you have believed, let it be done for you. Matt. 8:13

How do I rise and heal when all my hopes, dreams, and goals died with my loved one?

Beloved, My eye remains on you. You are never forgotten. How can I forget My own creation? Not only are you chosen, but I hold your destiny in My hand. Your name is tattooed on the palm of My hand. I will bind you up and make you well again. I will guide you through this difficult time, comfort you, and console you. All will be well wherever you are. While I live in high and holy places, I am also with you in your low and crushed spirit. I will put a new spirit within you and heal, lead, and comfort you. You are chosen, and your potential is limitless.

Write down your vision on tablets so anyone who reads it may follow it. The vision points ahead to an appointed time. Even if there is a delay, wait for it. It is coming and will come without delay. It can hardly wait. It is on its way. It will arrive right on time. Agree with My word and allow your faith to speak. Speak like Me, think like Me, and act like Me. Let your faith resonate powerfully. It is

a powerful force that can move mountains. Focus on what is true, noble, proper, pure, lovely, and admirable. You can do all things because I am with you and strengthen you. Then make your plans, and count on Me to direct you and make it happen.

I write to remind you to stir up the gift of God. I did not give you a cowardly spirit but a powerful, loving, and disciplined spirit. My gift of faith is like a flame, and when the embers of the fire have cooled, you must fan them again and keep them ablaze. My peace, I leave with you; My peace, I give you. Do not let your heart be troubled, and do not be afraid. Be bold. Be confident. Be courageous. Do not just sit there. Stir up the power. ARISE and TAKE decisive ACTION. Expect a harvest because you have the power to shape your future with your thoughts and words.

Scriptures: IS 44:21; IS 49:16; 1 Pet. 1:1-2; IS 57:18-19; HAB 2:2-3; 2 Tim. 1:6-9; Prov. 16:9; Phil 4:8-13

TODAY'S REFLECTION

WHAT IS YOUR POSITIVE THOUGHT FOR THE DAY?

WHAT ARE YOU GRATEFUL FOR TODAY?

WHAT ARE TODAY'S GOALS?

TODAY'S REFLECTION (CON'T)

WHAT WILL YOU GIVE UP TO ACCOMPLISH YOUR GOAL(S)?

WHAT IS GOD SAYING TO YOU TODAY?

WHAT GROWTH DID YOU EXPERIENCE TODAY?

Day 21

Rest and Recover

Anoint them with gladness instead of sorrow.

Isaiah 61:3

Lord, I can't sleep. Memories and dreams weigh heavily on my heart, reminding me of what once was.

Remember, I am your Creator, Shepherd, Redeemer, and Savior. I am always watching over you, never sleeping or slumbering. It is my privilege to grant sweet sleep to those I love. I will soothe your fears, keep count of your tossing and turnings, and even place your tears in my bottle. You are never alone. Lie down, My child, and sleep, for I will keep you safe. When you lie down, do not be afraid. I am the Eternal Shepherd, and I care for you always. I provide rest in rich, green fields beside streams of refreshing water. Trust in me, for I will make you whole again. I will guide you off rocky, challenging paths, steering you in the right direction.

I am with you in dark moments, near you, for your protection and guidance. Remember, healing from grief is a process, and you are making progress. Remain comforted by Me throughout this journey. It is okay to feel the way you do. Even though on the outside it looks

like things are falling apart, on the inside, God is creating a new life for you. Not a day goes by without My unfolding grace helping you navigate these circumstances and adapt to your new routine as you rebuild. Your tears will lessen, your anger will fade, and joy will greet you when you take a step forward.

Remember, do not set your sights on the things you can see with your eyes. All of that is fleeting; it will eventually fade away. Instead, focus on the things you cannot see, which live on eternally. You have reason to despair but do not despair. We do not sorrow or grieve like those who have no hope. Your loved one, who confessed Jesus Christ as Lord and Savior, is now present with the Lord. To be absent from the body is to be present with the Lord. This is the promise of eternal life, a hope that shines brighter than any darkness you will ever face.

Scriptures: PS. 56:8-9; PS. 121:4; PS. 4:8; Ps. 127:2; PS. 23; 2 Cor. 5:8; 2 Thess. 4:13-18

TODAY'S REFLECTION

WHAT IS YOUR POSITIVE THOUGHT FOR THE DAY?

WHAT ARE YOU GRATEFUL FOR TODAY?

WHAT ARE TODAY'S GOALS?

TODAY'S REFLECTION (CON'T)

WHAT WILL YOU GIVE UP TO ACCOMPLISH YOUR GOAL(S)?

WHAT IS GOD SAYING TO YOU TODAY?

WHAT GROWTH DID YOU EXPERIENCE TODAY?

Day 22

Empowered from Within

Be supernaturally infused with strength through your life-union with the Lord Jesus. Stand victorious with the force of His explosive power flowing in and through you.

Ephesians 6:10 TPT

I carry deep guilt and regrets about my loss, accompanied by great sorrow and unceasing anguish in my heart, along with tormenting unanswered questions that plague me.

As a merciful God, I heal the brokenhearted and bind your wounds. I am not only close to the brokenhearted, but I also rescue those crushed in spirit. Though weeping may endure for a night, joy surely comes in the morning. Even in your brokenness, I am the source of your strength, fully committed to your recovery. Pour out your heart before Me, and you will find solace in Me, a refuge and a hiding place for all who seek it. Prayer, praise, and petition can dispel the spirit of heaviness. Embrace gratitude and thanksgiving, then. My peace, which surpasses all understanding, will guard your heart and mind.

Be strong and courageous in the face of fear. Are you weary, worn out, or burned out? Come to Me. Spend time with Me, and you will recover your life and find restoration for your soul. Walk with Me and work with Me—watch how I do it and learn the unforced rhythms of grace. I will not lay anything heavy or ill-fitting on you. Keep company with Me, and you will learn to live freely and lightly. You should greatly rejoice in what is waiting for you, even if now, for a little while, you have to suffer various trials. Suffering tests your faith, which is more valuable than gold (remember that gold, although it is perishable), is tested by fire. If your faith is found genuine, your future victory is not just a possibility but a certainty, firm, steadfast, and immovable, so you are not tossed back and forth by your emotions and feelings. Remain anchored in me, and do not lose heart. The promise of a brighter future awaits you.

Scriptures: PS. 147:3; PS. 31:19; PS 34:18; PS. 30:5; PS. 73:26; PS. 62:8; Phil. 4:6-7; Matt. 11:28-30; 1 Cor. 15:58; 2 Cor. 4:16

TODAY'S REFLECTION

WHAT IS YOUR POSITIVE THOUGHT FOR THE DAY?

WHAT ARE YOU GRATEFUL FOR TODAY?

WHAT ARE TODAY'S GOALS?

TODAY'S REFLECTION (CON'T)

WHAT WILL YOU GIVE UP TO ACCOMPLISH YOUR GOAL(S)?

WHAT IS GOD SAYING TO YOU TODAY?

WHAT GROWTH DID YOU EXPERIENCE TODAY?

Day 23

First Things First

**In everything you do, put God first, and He will direct you and crown your efforts with success.
Prov. 3:6**

How do I find meaning and purpose in my life again?

Do not fear the future. Embrace it with confidence. I will heal the shattered wounds of your heart with unwavering compassion and love. I will turn your sorrow into joy! I take away your clothes of mourning and clothed you with joy. Only goodness and tender love shall pursue you throughout your life. I shaped you, inside and out. I knitted you together in your mother's womb long before you took your first breath. I see all things; nothing about you is hidden from Me. I carefully crafted you in your mother's womb. I see everything; I have already written every detail of your life in My book. I established the length of your life before you ever tasted the sweetness of it. I am committed to your well-being and will stand by your side.

Do not let go of My hand. My words are a flashlight to light the path ahead of you and keep You from stumbling. Create new goals that inspire you. I blessed you with certain gifts and talents for your personal

benefit. Make sure you utilize your gifts and talents effectively to help uplift others. This will help you connect and forge new relationships that enrich your life. Explore new activities and hobbies with great enthusiasm. Also, remain devoted to Me and search for Me with all your heart while focusing on the future and creating a new, inspiring narrative.

Be strong. Continue to be brave, and do not lose courage because your actions will reap rewards. I will make you successful. This hope is a strong and trustworthy anchor for your soul. Do not waver at My promises through unbelief, but be strengthened in faith, giving glory to Me; I cannot break My word. And because My word cannot change, the promise is likewise unchangeable. It is a rock-solid guarantee for your future life.

Scriptures: Ps. 23:6; Matt. 14:14; Ps. 139; Ps. 30:11; Ps. 147:3; Ps. 119:105; 1 Pet. 4:10; 2 Chron. 15:7; Rom. 4:20; Heb. 6:13-18

TODAY'S REFLECTION

WHAT IS YOUR POSITIVE THOUGHT FOR THE DAY?

WHAT ARE YOU GRATEFUL FOR TODAY?

WHAT ARE TODAY'S GOALS?

TODAY'S REFLECTION (CON'T)

WHAT WILL YOU GIVE UP TO ACCOMPLISH YOUR GOAL(S)?

WHAT IS GOD SAYING TO YOU TODAY?

WHAT GROWTH DID YOU EXPERIENCE TODAY?

Day 24

Choose Joy

Count it all joy
James 1:2

Today is the day I choose to rejoice. I will not be afraid. I will only believe.

When you trust in Me, I will make your joy complete. My arms are wide open so you can run to Me for safety, and you will be glad you did. You will break out in joyful song because I kept you safe. Then your love for Me will resound powerfully in your heart. I will show you the path of life; in My presence is fullness of joy, and at My right hand, there are pleasures forevermore. My revelation is whole and will pull your life back together again. My signposts are clear, pointing out the right path and road to take. My life maps are correct, showing the way to joy. My directions are straightforward and easy to follow. My reputation is like twenty-four-carat gold and comes with a lifetime guarantee.

It is impossible to please Me apart from faith. And why? Because anyone who wants to approach Me must believe that I exist and care enough to respond to those who seek Me. My commands are not burdensome. They lead to healing, victory, and peace. Be diligent to enter

into My rest. I have told you these things so that you may have perfect peace and confidence in Me. In this world, you will have tribulation, trials, distress, and frustration, but be of good cheer, take courage, be confident, certain, and undaunted! For I have overcome the world. I have deprived it of the power to harm you and have conquered it for you, bringing you the joy and peace that only faith can bring.

Be cheerful no matter what; Be happy in your faith, rejoice, and cultivate a continually grateful heart. Pray without ceasing. Praying persistently. Thank God, no matter what happens. No matter what the circumstances may be, be thankful and give thanks, for this is the will of God for you who are in Christ Jesus. Trust in Me. I will never fail or let you down.

Scriptures: Mark 5:36; Ps. 118:24; Deut. 16:15; Ps. 5:11; Ps. 16:11; Ps. 19:8-9; Heb. 11:6; Deut. 30:11; Heb. 4:11; 1 Thess. 5:17-18

TODAY'S REFLECTION

WHAT IS YOUR POSITIVE THOUGHT FOR THE DAY?

WHAT ARE YOU GRATEFUL FOR TODAY?

WHAT ARE TODAY'S GOALS?

TODAY'S REFLECTION (CON'T)

WHAT WILL YOU GIVE UP TO ACCOMPLISH YOUR GOAL(S)?

WHAT IS GOD SAYING TO YOU TODAY?

WHAT GROWTH DID YOU EXPERIENCE TODAY?

Day 25

Improve the Quality Of Your Life

"May God, the source of hope, fill you with joy and peace through your faith in him. Then you will overflow with hope by the power of the Holy Spirit." GNT
Romans 15:13

God, bitterness consumes my soul. I am angry and resentful because this is so incredibly unfair. What did I do to deserve this?

Watch out that no poisonous root of bitterness grows deep within you. When it springs up, this poison will cause you to miss My best blessings, such as peace, joy, and a sense of purpose. Bitterness will hurt your spiritual life, prayer life, and your relationship with Me. It will steal your joy and peace and rob you of my plan for your life. It will destroy your authority, anointing, dominion, destiny, purpose, and My will for your life. It will even delay your healing.

Get over yourself and this victim mentality. You are not a victim. You are not powerless. Stop blaming others for your situation. You are vulnerable and open to an attack from the enemy, the devil, who will tear you apart. You have become like a broken-down city without walls,

which makes you an easy target for the devil's attacks because you have no defense or protection. You must become well balanced (temperate, sober of mind), vigilant, and always cautious because your enemy, the devil, roams around like a lion seeking whom he may devour.

Remember, I have never lost a battle. My anointing rests upon you, giving you the strength and courage to stand your ground as boldly as a lion. So, get a firm grip on your faith and progressively operate in the fruit of the spirit: love, joy, peace, patience, kindness, goodness, faithfulness, gentleness, and self-control. This suffering won't last forever; you are not alone in this battle. I shall deliver you.

Scriptures: Heb. 12:15; 1 Pet. 5:8; Gal. 5:22-23

TODAY'S REFLECTION

WHAT IS YOUR POSITIVE THOUGHT FOR THE DAY?

WHAT ARE YOU GRATEFUL FOR TODAY?

WHAT ARE TODAY'S GOALS?

TODAY'S REFLECTION (CON'T)

WHAT WILL YOU GIVE UP TO ACCOMPLISH YOUR GOAL(S)?

WHAT IS GOD SAYING TO YOU TODAY?

WHAT GROWTH DID YOU EXPERIENCE TODAY?

Day 26

Change Course

Do you want to be made whole?
John 5:6

What will my life look like now? Everything feels so different, and I feel lost and very unsure.

My child, change has arrived. Trust in My divine guidance from the bottom of your heart; do not try to figure out everything on your own. Listen for My voice in everything you do and everywhere you go. I am the one who will keep you on track. Do not assume that you know it all. Run to Me! Those who set their minds on Me will be kept completely whole and steady because they persevere and do not quit. Your spiritual growth is a testament to your strength and resilience. Depend on Me, and keep at it because, in Me, you have a sure thing. Your actions and decisions play a crucial role in your success. Trust in My plan and not your own abilities.

I prophesy over you: change course, and I will transform your life. The old has gone; the new is here! Change course, and I will show up and take care of you as I promised. Change course; I know what I'm doing. I have

it all planned out—plans to take care of you, not abandon you, to give you the future you hope for. You possess the strength and resilience to overcome any challenge. You will emerge renewed! I will satisfy you with a long life and show you My salvation. You will have good success in life. Change course, and you will be compensated for your losses. You will witness the Lord's goodness in your lifetime: wholeness, healing, victory, freedom, peace, and joy—total restoration in your mind, body, and spirit. I will encourage, equip, and empower you.

Change course and keep your focus on me, and I will be your unwavering confidence, steadfast and strong, guarding you from hidden traps and dangers. Worship me in Spirit and truth. Worship me and watch me perform great and extraordinary wonders in your life right before your very eyes. And I will be that pillar in your life - unmovable and unshakeable.

Scriptures: Ps. 91:16; Josh. 1:8; Rom. 8:15; IS. 26:3-4; Jer 29:11; Ps. 27:13; Deut. 10:21; John 4:24; Prov. 3:26

TODAY'S REFLECTION

WHAT IS YOUR POSITIVE THOUGHT FOR THE DAY?

WHAT ARE YOU GRATEFUL FOR TODAY?

WHAT ARE TODAY'S GOALS?

TODAY'S REFLECTION (CON'T)

WHAT WILL YOU GIVE UP TO ACCOMPLISH YOUR GOAL(S)?

WHAT IS GOD SAYING TO YOU TODAY?

WHAT GROWTH DID YOU EXPERIENCE TODAY?

Day 27

An Unbreakable Spiritual Lifeline

This hope [this confident assurance] we have as an anchor of the soul [it cannot slip and it cannot break down under whatever pressure bears upon it]—a safe and steadfast hope that enters within the veil [of the heavenly temple, that most Holy Place in which the very presence of God dwells],
Hebrew 6:19

God, when will this storm end? I never saw this storm coming, and my soul is weary with sorrow; strengthen me according to Your word. I will dwell in the secret place of the Most-High and abide under the shadow of the Almighty. You are a shelter and shade from the day's heat and a refuge and hiding place from the storm and rain. Speak to my storm and command it to cease so calmness will reign in my life. Set me high upon a rock.

I am allowing your endurance a chance to grow. When your endurance is fully developed, you will be perfect and complete, needing nothing. Your endurance will allow you to navigate life's storm regardless of whatever stage you are in the process. Please do not lose hope because I am with you wherever you go. I, the Lord, have kept every promise I made to you. Not one of them has been broken.

My promises endure, and everything I have promised will come to pass, providing you with a sense of reassurance and security.

I will counsel you with my eye and instruct you in the night seasons. Set me always before you, and I will remain at your right hand forever. I will not be moved. I have laid a firm, solid foundation —a valuable cornerstone that has proven trustworthy. No one who trusts me will ever be disappointed. Trust in me, for I am your rock and your salvation. Now, may the God of all hope fill You with all joy and peace as you trust in Him so that you may overflow with hope and optimism by the power of the Holy Spirit.

Scriptures: PS. 91: 1; IS 4:6; PS 27:5; JM. 1:4; Josh. 1:9; Josh 21:45; PS. 32:8; PS. 16:8; IS 28:16-23; PS. 62:2; Rom. 15:13

TODAY'S REFLECTION

WHAT IS YOUR POSITIVE THOUGHT FOR THE DAY?

WHAT ARE YOU GRATEFUL FOR TODAY?

WHAT ARE TODAY'S GOALS?

TODAY'S REFLECTION (CON'T)

WHAT WILL YOU GIVE UP TO ACCOMPLISH YOUR GOAL(S)?

WHAT IS GOD SAYING TO YOU TODAY?

WHAT GROWTH DID YOU EXPERIENCE TODAY?

Day 28

Mindset Shift

Casting down arguments and every high thing that exalts itself against the knowledge of God, bringing every thought into captivity to the obedience of Christ. **2 Cor. 10:5**

How long will my loss trigger me, God? People, places, things, circumstances, and words often trigger me. It is only natural for me to feel the way I do, as some of these memories may or may not have a special place in my heart. However, these triggers often cause me to weep and spiral out of control in my emotions. Sometimes, I cannot sleep.

So, here's what I'm going to do. I will help you: Embracing what I have done for you is the best thing you can do. Fix your attention on Me, and I will heal you from the inside out. Readily recognize what I want from you and respond quickly. Take your everyday, ordinary life—your sleeping, eating, going to work, and walking around life—and place it before Me as an offering. I will bring out the best in you, and you will progress along in your grief.

Do not languish in this position. Instead of conforming to the world's ways of dealing with grief, allow Me to

transform you into a new person by reshaping your thoughts and responses to your emotions. Entrust every thought and feeling to Me. Then, you will discover My will for you, which is good, pleasing, and perfect, leading you to a hopeful and inspired future.

Let the peace that comes from Me reign in your heart, settling all the questions that arise in your mind. As the Lord of Peace (Jehovah Shalom), who lacks nothing and can mend all brokenness, I grant you My peace, the peace of My kingdom, at all times and in all ways, under all circumstances and conditions. Remember, I am with you always, providing you with a sense of security and support.

Scriptures: Rom. 12:1-2; Matt. 28:20; Col. 3:15; 2 Thes. 3:16;

TODAY'S REFLECTION

WHAT IS YOUR POSITIVE THOUGHT FOR THE DAY?

WHAT ARE YOU GRATEFUL FOR TODAY?

WHAT ARE TODAY'S GOALS?

TODAY'S REFLECTION (CON'T)

WHAT WILL YOU GIVE UP TO ACCOMPLISH YOUR GOAL(S)?

WHAT IS GOD SAYING TO YOU TODAY?

WHAT GROWTH DID YOU EXPERIENCE TODAY?

Day 29

Arise, Encourage, and Strengthen Yourself Take Off Your Grave Clothes

David encouraged and strengthened himself in the Lord his God.
1 Sam. 30:6 AMPC

What now? Where do I go from here? My heart is sad and discouraged from crying the blues. However, I refuse to stay in this place of self-pity. I will arise despite my bitter weeping, take off my grave clothes, and move on from this place of deep despair. My soul takes courage, and I boldly approach Your presence with thanksgiving and praise Your divine authority. I give thanks to You and praise Your name.

I will continually praise You because You are my helper. I worship you, Lord. I declare the works of the Lord. I worship and adore You. I put my hope in You! You put a smile on my face. You are my God. You restore my soul. Your praise shall continually be in my mouth. You put a new song in my mouth, a hymn of praise to my God, lifting me up with Your presence.

You, LORD, are my shield, my glory, the lifter of my head. Guide me in Your ways, for I trust in Your wisdom. You make firm the steps of those who delight in You. I will

not fear, for You are with me; I will not be dismayed, for You are my God, my protector. Strengthen me, uphold me with Your righteous hand.

You are my strength and my support, no matter where my journey takes me and how low I may feel. Therefore, I worship You in spirit and truth. You reign over all the earth. You are Holy. Holy, holy, holy is the Lord God Almighty who was, and is, and is to come. You give strength to Your people, and You bless Your people with peace.

Scriptures: Ps. 23:3; Ps. 42:5; Ps. 34:17; Ps. 34:1; Ps. 40:3; Ps. 3:3; Ps. 32:8; Ps. 37:23; IS 41:10; John 4:23; Rev. 4:8; Ps. 29:11;

TODAY'S REFLECTION

WHAT IS YOUR POSITIVE THOUGHT FOR THE DAY?

WHAT ARE YOU GRATEFUL FOR TODAY?

WHAT ARE TODAY'S GOALS?

TODAY'S REFLECTION (CON'T)

WHAT WILL YOU GIVE UP TO ACCOMPLISH YOUR GOAL(S)?

WHAT IS GOD SAYING TO YOU TODAY?

WHAT GROWTH DID YOU EXPERIENCE TODAY?

Day 30

Anointed With Fresh Oil

"May the God of hope fill you with all joy and peace as you trust in Him, so that you may overflow with hope by the power of the Holy Spirit."
Romans 15:13

Now, you are anointed with fresh oil, a powerful symbol of the Holy Spirit's strength, to conquer and overcome sadness, loneliness, anxiety, and depression. Because you are righteous, you shall flourish like a palm tree - solid, strong, immovable, and filled with the Holy Spirit's empowering presence. When the Holy Spirit has come upon you, you shall receive power and be witnesses to Me to the end of the earth. You shall grow like a cedar in Lebanon and remain planted in the house of the Lord. You shall flourish in My courts and bear fresh, flourishing fruit. Allow the Holy Spirit to dwell in you and be filled with the Spirit with the evidence of speaking in tongues. And then, when you Walk in the Spirit, you will not fulfill the lust of the flesh or succumb to feelings of dejection, sorrow, despondency, and melancholy. Where the Spirit of the Lord is, there is liberty.

Remain united with Christ in your heart, just as the Spirit has taught you to do. Get unstuck. It is really easy to feel

sorry for yourself and fall into self-pity. That is why I remind you to stir up (rekindle the embers of, fan the flame of, and keep burning) the gracious gift of God, [the inner fire] that is in you, stay one in your heart with Christ, just as the Spirit has taught you to do. Arise, why are you still sitting here? Do you want to be made well? Do you want to be healed? Remember, healing and recovery are not just possibilities; they are promises. You will reclaim your life—keep your eyes forward and your feet in motion. Be courageous and take a chance. Bounce back. When good people are down, they get back up every time. All things are possible with ME.

Scriptures: Ps. 92; Acts 1:8; Gal. 5:16; 2 Cor. 3:17; Eph 4:1-6; 2 Tim. 1:6; 2 King 7; Prov. 24:16

TODAY'S REFLECTION

WHAT IS YOUR POSITIVE THOUGHT FOR THE DAY?

WHAT ARE YOU GRATEFUL FOR TODAY?

WHAT ARE TODAY'S GOALS?

TODAY'S REFLECTION (CON'T)

WHAT WILL YOU GIVE UP TO ACCOMPLISH YOUR GOAL(S)?

WHAT IS GOD SAYING TO YOU TODAY?

WHAT GROWTH DID YOU EXPERIENCE TODAY?

Receive Jesus As Your Savior

Accepting Jesus as your personal Lord and Savior will be the best decision you can make with your life.

Scripture says, *"If you openly declare that Jesus is Lord and believe in your heart that God raised him from the dead, you will be saved. For it is by believing in your heart that you are made right with God, and it is by openly declaring your faith that you are saved. As the Scriptures tell us, "Anyone who trusts in him will never be disgraced." For "Everyone who calls on the name of the Lord will be saved (Rom. 10:9-13)."*

Pray out loud:

"God, our heavenly Father, you said anyone who confesses You as Lord and Savior and believes in their heart that You raised Him from the dead shall be saved. I confess You as my Lord and Savior. I ask you to forgive me of all my sins and come into my heart. I am saved by faith, cleansed by faith, and made a new creature in Jesus Christ by faith. Thank you, Father, in Jesus' Name. Amen."

Congratulations! I encourage you to find and join a Bible-believing, Bible-teaching church where you can experience exponential growth. I recommend Faith City Central. You can learn more about them by visiting their website: https://faithcitycentral.org/

Receive the Holy Spirit

After accepting Jesus Christ as your personal Lord and Savior, you need to be equipped and empowered by the Holy Spirit. The following scriptures support receiving the Holy Spirit's indwelling.

Acts 1:8

New King James Version

"But you shall receive power when the Holy Spirit has come upon you, and you shall be witnesses to Me in Jerusalem, and in all Judea and Samaria, and to the end of the earth."

Luke 11:9-13

New King James Version

"So, I say to you, ask, and it will be given to you; seek, and you will find; knock, and it will be opened to you. For everyone who asks receives, and he who seeks finds, and to him who knocks, it will be opened...How much more will *your* heavenly Father give the Holy Spirit to those who ask Him!"

Now, all you have to do is ask, receive, and believe that you receive.

Pray Out Loud:

"Father, I need to be equipped and empowered by Your Holy Spirit. I ask you to fill me with the Holy Spirit with the evidence of speaking in other tongues. According to Luke 11:9-13, you said, ask, and it will be given to anyone who asks and who receives. Father, I thank you that I am now filled and baptized with Your Holy Spirit with the evidence of speaking in other tongues. Amen."

After you pray, take a deep breath, make a sound with your voice, move your tongue and lips, and speak your heavenly language. Syllables will rise up from within you. Because you asked in faith, believe that you receive regardless of whether you spoke today. (Mark 11:24)

Endnotes

Abeles, M., & Katz, J. S. (2010). A Time To Mourn: Reflections on Jewish Bereavement Practices. *Bereavement Care, 29*(1), 19-22.

Howarth, R. A. (2011). Concepts and Controversies In Grief And Loss. *Journal Of Mental Health Counseling, 33*(1), 4-10.

Iwanowska, J., & Rucińska, M. (2024). Death, Burial, and Mourning in Judaism. *Palliative Medicine in Practice, (18)2:* 75–81

Kübler-Ross, E., & Kessler, D. (2009). The Five Stages of Grief. In *Library of Congress Catalogin in publication data (Ed.), on Grief and Grieving* (pp. 7-30).

Laurence, M. & Welkart, R. (1984). Loss, Grief, Mourning: *What to Do. Can. Fam. Physician, 30,* 669-673.

Pop-Jordanova, N. (2021). Grief: Etiology, Symptoms, and Management. P*rilozi, 42*(2), 9-18.

Saxey, M. (2020). Empathy v. Sympathy: Are My Attempts Really Helping Others? *Family Perspectives, 2*(1), 7.

https://www.peoples-law.org/powers-attorney.

https://www.marylandattorneygeneral.gov/Pages/HealthPolicy/AdvanceDirectives.aspx

Unless otherwise noted, all scriptures are taken from https://www.biblegateway.com/ and include scriptures from the following biblical versions:

- Amplified Bible (AMP)
- Amplified Bible, Classic Edition (AMPC)
- Common English Bible (CEB)
- Contemporary English Version (CEV)
- Easy-to-Read Version (ERV)
- EasyEnglish Bible (EASY)
- English Standard Version (ESV)
- Living Bible (TLB)
- The Message (MSG)
- New American Standard Bible (NASB)
- New International Version (NIV)
- New King James Version (NKJV)
- New Living Translation (NLT)
- The Voice (VOICE)

About the Author

Dr. Digna Wheatley Pearson is a licensed minister at Faith City Central, where she has served for over 18 years. A native of the United States Virgin Islands, Digna is a woman after God's heart who chooses to embrace God's plans for her life by devoting her time and energy to serving others.

Digna combines her passion for God with a distinguished healthcare career. She has been a registered nurse in the healthcare industry for over twenty years. Digna brings nearly sixteen years of invaluable experience in Quality, Patient Relations, Risk Management, and Regulatory Affairs at the Johns Hopkins Health System. She is currently serving as a driving force, making valuable contributions in Service Excellence, specifically in the realm of Patient Experience. She is also a certified professional in healthcare risk management. Digna holds a Doctorate in Strategic Leadership from Regent University with a concentration in Leadership Coaching, a Master's in Biblical and Theological Studies from Dallas Theological Seminary, a Master of Health Administration, a Bachelor of Science in Nursing, and a Bachelor of Arts in Health Administration from the University of Maryland.

In her native hometown, a high school gymnasium proudly bears her name, honoring her leadership in spearheading a march for educational equality. This march resulted in the construction of 12 classrooms, a gymnasium, a bus shed, a track and field, the purchase of textbooks, and the recruitment of teachers.

Dr. Wheatley-Pearson resides in the beautiful state of Maryland. Her daughter, Taylor, a healthcare attorney, is the absolute love of her life.

Contact Information

Website: https://www.dignifiedsolutionz.com/

Email: dignifiedsolutionz@gmail.com

Books by Dr. Digna Wheatley Pearson

Elevation: Empowering and Equipping the Church for Excellence By Creating A Coaching Culture and Using High-Reliability Principles

Crown of Life Confessions

Anchored in Hope: Good Grief Devotional Journal

References

_____

[i] Howarth, R. A. (2011). Concepts and Controversies In Grief And Loss. *Journal Of Mental Health Counseling*, *33*(1), 4-10.

[ii] Ibid.

[iii] Ibid.

[iv] Kübler-Ross, E., & Kessler, D. (2009). The Five Stages Of Grief. In *Library of Congress Catalogin in publication data (Ed.), on grief and grieving* (pp. 7-30).

[v] Ibid.

[vi] Iwanowska, J., & Rucińska, M. (2024). Death, Burial, and Mourning in Judaism. *Palliative Medicine in Practice, (18)2:* 75–81

[vii] Ibid.

[viii] Ibid.

[ix] Ibid.

[x] https://www.nia.nih.gov/health/grief-and-mourning/coping-grief-and-loss

[xi] https://www.peoples-law.org/powers-attorney.

[xii] Ibid.

[xiii] https://www.marylandattorneygeneral.gov/Pages/HealthPolicy/AdvanceDirectives.aspx

[xiv] Pearson, D. (2025). Christian Counseling II [PowerPoint presentation]. Faith City Bible Institute.

[xv] Saxey, M. (2020). Empathy v. Sympathy: Are My Attempts Really Helping Others? *Family Perspectives*, *2*(1), 7.